Hate

Perspectives on Violence

by Gus Gedatus

Consultant:
Dr. Michael Obsatz
Associate Professor of Sociology
Macalester College, St. Paul, Minnesota

LifeMatters
an imprint of Capstone Press
Mankato, Minnesota

LifeMatters Books are published by Capstone Press
PO Box 669 • 151 Good Counsel Drive • Mankato, Minnesota 56002
http://www.capstone-press.com

Printed in the United States of America

Library of Congress Cataloging-in-Publication Data
Gedatus, Mark Gustav.
     Hate / by Gus Gedatus.
         p.   cm. — (Perspectives on violence)
     Includes bibliographical references and index.
     Summary: Describes various aspects of hate crimes including the victims, perpetrators, their effects, and ways to combat them.
     ISBN 0-7368-0427-7 (book) — 0-7368-0439-0 (series)
     1. Hate crimes—United States—Juvenile literature. 2. Victims of crime—United States—Juvenile literature. 3. Crime prevention—United States—Juvenile literature. [1. Hate crimes. 2. Victims of crime. 3. Crime prevention.] I. Title. II. Series.
     HV6773.52.G44 2000
     364.1—dc21
                                    99-056216
                                    CIP

Staff Credits
Charles Pederson, editor; Adam Lazar, designer; Jodi Theisen, photo researcher

Photo Credits
Cover: The Stock Market/©John Henley, large; PNI/©Paul Miller, small
FPG/9; ©VCG, 32; ©Kevin Laubacher, 49
International Stock/©Will Stanton, 7; ©R. Pharaoh, 17; ©Scott Barrow, 18; ©Michael Paras, 37; ©Scott Barrow, 57
Photo Network/©Myrleen Cate, 22; ©Eric R. Berndt, 44; ©Jeff Greenberg, 55
Photri/©MacDonald Photograpy, 8; ©Skjold, 15
Picture Cube/©Rick Scott, 24
Unicorn/©Jeff Greenberg, 39; ©Jim Shippee, 46
Uniphoto/©Ed Elberfeld, 43
Visuals Unlimited/©Jeff Greenberg, 59

Table of Contents

Chapter Overview

Hate crimes are a form of violence aimed at people of a particular national origin. Race, religion, disability, sexual orientation, and gender are other reasons people are targeted. People who are different from the majority group may be targets of hate.

Genocide is a planned attempt to kill an entire group or race of people.

International conditions can influence hate crimes against particular groups.

Chapter 1

What Is Hate?

Violence is words or actions that hurt people or the things they care about. Hate crimes are acts of violence aimed at people because of their national origin. Race, religion, disability, and gender, or sex, are other reasons people become targets of hate. Another reason is sexual orientation. This is someone's sexual attraction to, behavior toward, or desire for another person based on gender.

"Congress shall make no law ... abridging the freedom of speech."—First Amendment to the Constitution of the United States

Individual American states and Canadian provinces define hate crimes differently. Some have stiff penalties for these crimes. Recently, the U.S. Supreme Court defined hate crimes as criminal acts ranging from vandalism to murder. Vandalism is needless destruction of property. Hate crimes often follow hate speech, which is spoken or printed insults against certain groups of people. Section II of the Canadian Charter of Rights and Freedoms protects the right to hate speech. The First Amendment to the U.S. Constitution does the same thing. However, neither country gives the right to commit hate crimes.

How Many Hate Crimes Are There?

Experts believe that between 10,000 and 40,000 hate crimes are committed each year in the United States. Not all of these crimes are reported. According to the Federal Bureau of Investigation (FBI), 8,049 hate crimes were reported in the United States in 1997. Since then, experts believe the number of hate crimes has decreased. White people commit about 60 percent of all hate crimes.

Perpetrators, or people who commit hate crimes, often don't seek to harm just one person. They want to intimidate, or bully, an entire group. The victims have done nothing to deserve the violence. They may simply look different or have different beliefs, behaviors, or background from those who commit hate crimes.

People who are different from perpetrators often are the victims of hate. For example, residents of a certain place may fear or hate strangers or foreigners. This fear may cause the residents to act out violently against the strangers or foreigners. Some people who hate may think they have a mission to get rid of people who are different. Also, when minority groups become more visible, hate crimes against them frequently increase. This may happen because the members of the majority group feel threatened.

While many people hate, it is important to realize that hate can be overcome. People can learn to accept and understand others and to value their differences. This book describes some of the reasons for hate and the people who hate. It also describes some ways that organizations and individuals can work to counter hate.

Genocide

One certain kind of hate crime called genocide is the intentional murder of an entire group or race. It is an attempt to get rid of everyone who is different from the majority group.

Genocide has been practiced throughout the world at different times. During World War II, for example, the German leader was Adolf Hitler. He created and carried out a plan to kill more than six million Jews and others. During the 1990s, Serb soldiers in the former Yugoslavia tried to rid the region of Muslims and Croats. Sometimes the Muslims and Croats took revenge against the Serbs with their own hate crimes. Tens of thousands of people died in the Yugoslavian region as a result of genocide. In 1994, the Hutu people of Rwanda set out to kill their Tutsi enemies. Over several months, more than 500,000 people were killed.

Unfortunately, genocide still happens in some parts of the world.

International Influences on Hate Crimes at Home

International conditions may cause an increase in hate crimes against certain groups at home. For instance, some Japanese car models outsold U.S. models in the 1980s. Many people worried that Japanese products would cause North American workers to lose their jobs. For this reason, Japanese people in North America became the targets of hate crimes for a time.

In the early 1990s, Canadian and U.S. soldiers fought with other countries in the Gulf War. The enemy was Iraq, an Arab country. During that time, Arabs in North America were sometimes the victims of hate crimes. The victims were not always Iraqis. Their businesses and places of worship were sometimes vandalized or destroyed. After the war, hate crimes against Arabs decreased.

Points to Consider

Do you think hate speech should be protected by law? Why or why not?

Do you agree that genocide has not occurred for many years in the United States or Canada? Why or why not?

How do you feel when you hear or read about a hate crime that has been committed?

Chapter
Overview

Immigrants are common targets of hate. They often are easy to identify.

Hate crimes are often committed against members of racial or religious minority groups.

Sexual orientation and gender are sometimes the basis for hate.

Chapter **2**

Who Is Hated?

Many groups and individual group members are targeted for hate. Almost always the perpetrators of hate consider the victims to be strangers or outsiders. In the United States and Canada, immigrants and members of particular racial or ethnic groups are targeted. Many religious groups and people with a different sexual orientation also are targeted. Crimes based on gender are sometimes considered hate crimes, too, though not by law.

He prayed; it wasn't my religion.

He ate; it wasn't what I ate.

He spoke; it wasn't my language.

He dressed; it wasn't what I wore.

He took my hand; it wasn't the color of mine.

But when he laughed, it was how I laughed,

and when he cried, it was how I cried.

—Amy Maddox, Bargersville, Indiana

Immigrants

Immigrants are common targets of hate crimes. They often are easy to identify as being different. They might look, dress, or talk differently from other people in an area. They might not speak the local language well. They may live in an easily identified area. They may be poor and not allowed to vote. For these reasons, they may have a hard time getting needed help or attention.

Racial and Ethnic Groups

Most hate crimes in the United States and Canada are directed at members of racial and ethnic groups. People of African, Asian, and Hispanic backgrounds are often victims. Even white people are the victims of hate crimes.

In the United States, most hate crimes are against African Americans. They are the victims of almost 40 percent of hate crimes. The enslavement of Africans until the end of the American Civil War in 1865 set a pattern of discrimination. Many people accepted or practiced this poor treatment of others, which is based on prejudgments about others. Although the Civil War ended slavery, it did not end hate against African Americans. After the Civil War, organized hate groups committed many acts of violence against African Americans. For instance, between 1882 and 1892, 1,400 African Americans were illegally hanged. The criminals often went unpunished.

In 1997, the FBI recorded over 1,000 antiwhite crimes. That was about 16 percent of the total number of hate crimes.

Religious Groups

For centuries, most religious groups have been persecuted, or continually attacked and mistreated, at some time. For example, in the ancient Roman empire, Christians were harassed and killed. Religious persecution and mistreatment continue in many parts of the world. In North America today, hate groups continue to attack members of many religions.

One form of persecution is anti-Semitism. This hatred of Jews is an attitude that has been learned over centuries. It has existed throughout the history of Canada and the United States. Some non-Jewish European settlers in North America brought anti-Semitism to this continent. Some people still hold that attitude today. For example, a man shot three children and two adults at a Los Angeles Jewish community center in 1999. When the man was arrested, he said he wanted all Americans to kill Jews.

Jews are the victim of most hate crimes based on religion. In 1997, the FBI reported about 80 percent of U.S. hate crimes based on religion were against Jewish people. Most of these crimes involve vandalism to schools, cemeteries, and synagogues, or houses of worship. Jews report more vandalism than any other group.

Homosexual, Bisexual, and Transsexual People

Some people hate or fear homosexual, bisexual, or transsexual males and females. Homosexual people are attracted to people of the same gender. Bisexual people are attracted to both males and females. Homosexual males often are called gay, and homosexual females often are called lesbian. Some males feel like they are female, and some females feel like they are males. These are called transsexual people.

Recently, issues involving gay and lesbian people have provoked violence from people who fear homosexuality. Such issues are AIDS, legal recognition of same-sex partnerships, and gay people in the military. These issues have brought homosexuality into public awareness. As a result, hate crimes against gay, lesbian, and bisexual people rose sharply during the early 1990s. More than 1,100 hate crimes against homosexual, bisexual, and transsexual people were reported to the FBI in 1997. About 69 percent of these crimes were against gay males.

Martha and Hank were dating when they were 17. Shortly after **MARTHA, AGE 18** they started going steady, Hank started beating Martha. She found out that he used to beat other girls he dated.

Hank told Martha, "All girls need a good beating now and then. Otherwise, they get too full of themselves."

"Well, maybe that's how it is with some people," Martha replied. "But I am not putting up with it." Martha told Hank he had to promise never to hit her. When he refused, Martha broke up with him.

Females

Females are frequent targets of hate crimes. Hate crimes against females often involve assault, rape, or both. However, no organized hate groups are known to target females. Perpetrators are often individual males who hate females. For instance, in 1999, a Yosemite Park employee confessed to killing four women. He said that for years he had wanted to kill women. It didn't matter who they were, as long as they were women.

At present, laws against hate crimes don't cover females. The U.S. Congress is debating whether crimes against females should be included in federal hate crimes laws.

Points to Consider

·Why do you think so many hate crimes are aimed at people from ethnic or religious groups?

How are hate crimes against women different from crimes against members of other groups?

What would you do if you were a victim of a hate crime?

What would you tell someone who was a victim of a hate crime?

Chapter Overview

Ignorance, poverty, joblessness, or a failure to fit in are possible causes of hate.

Many hate groups exist. Among these groups are the Ku Klux Klan, Aryan Nations, and skinheads.

Perpetrators have used the Internet to spread their messages of hate. They believe the Internet is an effective way to gain new recruits.

Chapter **3**
The Perpetrators of Hate

When Vincent was 8, he played in a group that included a **VINCENT, AGE 17** Japanese boy and an African American boy. His father beat Vincent for playing with those two kids. Vincent never again played with people who were different from him.

In middle school, Vincent began to fight, usually because of name-calling. Shortly after he turned 17, Vincent was injured in a fight. He had told three Hispanic boys to go back where they came from.

Why People Hate

Experts have many ideas about why people hate those who are different. Many people believe a difference in lifestyle or language is the cause. Some experts blame poverty and joblessness for hate. At times, foreigners or strangers have been accused unfairly of taking jobs that natives of an area otherwise might have. People who commit hate crimes often feel superior to the people they hurt and kill.

Ignorance and fear play a large part in hate crimes. Others' differences may seem frightening to people who don't understand them. Stereotypes, which are overly simple ideas about an entire group, sometimes influence people to hate. Stereotypes can prevent people from thinking carefully about others. Instead, people may rely on what someone else says. When people see only others' differences, it can be easy not to think of them as individuals. For example, Adolf Hitler pointed at European Jews' differences and claimed that they were not human.

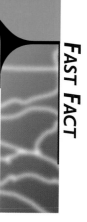
In Germany, hate crimes are called right-wing violence or xenophobic violence, which is violence against strangers. In England and France, they are called racial violence.

Hate Groups

Some hate groups purposely try to appeal to young people who may be angry. The groups may be successful, since people under age 18 commit about one-fourth of all hate crimes.

Hate groups can provide a place for some young people to fit in. Members may feel they must prove they are loyal group members by doing what the group wants. Otherwise, these young people might never consider committing violent acts of hatred.

Members of hate groups may think that only their beliefs and ideas are correct. These groups typically commit hate crimes against people of African descent. Jews and members of other religious groups, and gay and lesbian people are also commonly targeted.

One group that monitors hate group activities is the Southern Poverty Law Center (SPLC), in Montgomery, Alabama. The SPLC has identified 800 hate groups. The Anti-Defamation League (ADL) is another group that fights prejudice against Jews and all minority groups. Prejudice is an unfair opinion, or prejudgment, about a person or group before all the facts are known. The ADL has found that hate groups have about 15,000 members in 40 states. Experts believe that these groups are gaining strength largely through TV, radio, video, newspapers, and the Internet.

The Ku Klux Klan

One of the oldest hate groups in the United States is the Ku Klux Klan. Begun shortly after the Civil War, the Klan focused on intimidating newly freed African slaves. Klan members also spread a fear of immigrants. The Klan's hate list eventually included Catholics, Jews, and other minority groups, who were often poor immigrants. Today the Klan exists as more than 30 separate groups.

Klan members have been convicted of hate crimes against minority groups. For example, in the mid-1990s, several Klan members were arrested in connection with fires at African American churches.

The Aryan Nations

The Aryan Nations is a neo-Nazi hate group. Neo-Nazi means "new Nazi." These groups follow Hitler's ideas. According to Klanwatch, part of the SPLC, Aryan Nations is the fastest-growing hate group. Like many other organized hate groups, Aryan Nations aims to recruit young people ages 14 to 25.

Skinheads

Some hate groups are known as skinheads. This is because members closely shave and sometimes tattoo their heads. Some skinheads wear military-style clothing such as bomber jackets and combat boots. They are often neo-Nazis. Skinheads believe that white males are superior to other groups of people. They target members of many nonwhite, non-Protestant minority groups.

Benjamin Nathaniel Smith grew up in an average suburban family in Chicago. Smith's friends considered him intelligent and well read.

When Smith entered college, he had close friends in different groups. As time passed, Smith became distant. He started feeling that he couldn't trust people. His reading began to include books such as a biography of Adolf Hitler.

One day, Smith responded to a flyer that members of the World Church of the Creator left on his car. He met with a group leader who explained the church's beliefs. Its Golden Rule was: "What is good for the white race is good. What is bad for the white race is bad."

On the weekend of July 4, 1999, Smith shot nine Jews, Asians, and African Americans. Two of them died. Smith then killed himself. He had told friends that he didn't mind dying for a cause he believed in.

Hate on the Internet

In the past, hate groups recruited members at rallies or by passing out or mailing flyers to individuals. It was a slow process and attracted few new members. Hate groups' recruiting methods have changed with increased access to the Internet. In fact, the SPLC estimates that more than 250 hate groups have sites on the Internet.

The targets of Internet hate, however, have not changed. Targets range from African Americans to homosexual people to Jews. There are even Internet sites against doctors who help women have abortions. An abortion ends a pregnancy.

Points to Consider

Do you think fear is a reason people join hate groups? Why or why not?

Why do you think young people are attracted to hate groups?

Do you think people other than whites might have hate groups? Why or why not?

How would you feel if you were the target of a hate crime like vandalism?

How do you think the Internet can be used to fight hate groups?

Chapter Overview

Hate can have a ripple effect. The fear and anger that hate causes spread from the victim to family, friends, and neighborhoods.

Revenge for hate crimes only increases the violence.

The financial, social, and emotional costs of hate crimes are high.

Hate shuts down communication among groups as people stop trusting. It tends to break down people's sense of community.

Chapter **4**

The Effects of Hate

SAIED, AGE 15

Saied and his family were immigrants from Egypt. He spoke English well, got good grades in school, and was an excellent basketball player. Saied had lots of friends. Lately, people had made threats against Muslims. Anti-Islam messages had been spray-painted on the wall of the mosque where Saied's family prayed. Then someone set fire to the building. Saied's uncle Massout was cleaning in the basement when the fire started. He barely escaped.

After the fire, Saied didn't care much for school, his friends, or even basketball. Saied wondered why the city where he lived had so many people who hated.

"[The Nazis] first came for the Communists, and I didn't speak up because I wasn't a Communist. Then they came for the Jews, and I didn't speak up because I wasn't a Jew.... Then they came for the Catholics, and I didn't speak up because I was a Protestant. Then they came for me—and by that time no one was left to speak up."—German Pastor Martin Niemoeller

The Ripple Effect

When hate harms one person, the pain spreads to others like ripples in water. Family members and friends become angry and fearful. Members of the same race, ethnic group, or neighborhood may become afraid, too.

The ripple effect can spread to touch other people. Hate crimes against people of certain races or religions can bring back painful memories. For instance, a teen may see a news story about a hate group's meeting. The racist names that the group uses may cause the teen to remember being called similar names at school.

Police are expected to protect all members of a community equally. Occasionally, however, police have chosen to ignore hate crimes. When this happens, members of a victimized group may lose faith in police. They may believe that people from their group are not really protected. This ripple expands to include even more people.

A Cycle of Violence

After a hate crime, victims may feel afraid or angry. The fear and anger may start a cycle of increasing revenge and violence. Even if the victim doesn't want revenge, members of the victim's group may want it. The revenge might be against the perpetrators themselves. It might be against a member of the perpetrators' group. The revenge is often a crime in itself. It may cause the original perpetrators to become more angry and violent. They may take further revenge against their victim. This cycle of violence is often difficult to stop.

Many Costs

Like other crimes, hate crimes are costly in many ways. For example, more law enforcement officials and court staff may be needed. This may mean increased taxes. When victims are hurt, they need medical attention. They must pay medical fees, and their insurance rates may rise. Repairing property that vandals have damaged is expensive. All these things cost money.

Social and emotional costs are more difficult to measure. However, they are just as real as financial costs. For example, victims may feel people they thought were friends have betrayed them. Victims may become more distrusting of other people. The cycle of violence that hate creates can increase fear and distrust. Regaining trust among groups is difficult once fear takes hold. Individuals and society may end up paying for the effects of hate for a long time.

Unexpected Effects

Sometimes hate crimes may not have the effect that the perpetrators expected. Occasionally, hate crimes make people sad or angry enough to take action. For example, Matthew Shepard was an openly gay college student in Wyoming. In October 1998, he was tied to a fence, beaten, and burned. He died in a hospital several hours later. Two young men, Aaron McKinney and Russell Henderson, were arrested for the crime. They had killed Shepard because he was gay. They were convicted of Shepard's murder and sentenced to life in prison without possibility of early release.

Hate crimes are five times more likely than other crimes to involve assault.

Shepard's murder came to national attention. It renewed some people's belief that federal laws must include hate crimes based on sexual orientation. At present, federal laws don't cover crimes based on sexual orientation. The U.S. Congress is waiting to vote on an amended Hate Crimes Act. It would cover crimes based on sexual orientation.

Points to Consider

Do you think younger or older people have a harder time with the effects of hate crimes? Why?

Might a positive ripple effect against hate occur? Why or why not?

Do you think it is possible for a hate crime to have a positive outcome? Why or why not?

Chapter
Overview

There are many reasons people might not report hate crimes. However, individuals can make a difference in stopping hate when they report such crimes.

Hate crimes are not simply someone's mischief. They deeply hurt the victims.

If you are a victim of hate, you have many options for responding.

You can offer valuable support to victims of hate.

Chapter **5**

If You or Someone You Know Is a Victim of Hate

Why Hate Crimes Aren't Reported

Many hate crimes are believed to go unreported. There are many reasons for this. Victims may be afraid that their attackers will get back at them if the crime is reported. Some victims don't believe the perpetrators will be brought to justice. Other victims believe that describing their experience would be shameful. Some victims may not trust police because of bad experiences with them in the past. Immigrant victims of hate may not speak the local language well enough to report it.

"Silence encourages the tormentor, never the tormented."—Elie Wiesel

Today there are many good reasons why individuals can and should report hate crimes. Specific laws define what hate crimes are and how to punish them. Law enforcement agencies cooperate in North America and worldwide to catch perpetrators. Police and law enforcement people are better trained to deal with hate. Chances are, reporting a hate crime will make a difference.

If You Are a Victim

Hate crimes are not simply someone's mischief or the result of someone's careless fun. They have a deep and lasting effect on victims. For example, neo-Nazi symbols or a burning cross tell members of a group that they are not wanted alive. Victims of hate often feel alone and open to attack. However, they do have choices for responding to hate.

If you are ever the victim of a hate crime, only you can decide how to react. If you do decide to speak up, here are some steps to take.

Report every incident of hate directed toward you. Police and other law enforcement agencies are more willing than ever before to investigate hate crimes.

Ask for help from friends, neighbors, and the community. Also, many organizations exist to help fight hate crimes. Most people share an instinct for tolerance. Chances are, you will find many people who support you and will stand with you.

Write a letter to the editor. Your honest story in the news media can be a powerful motivator to others. Most likely, people will support and encourage you.

Seek out friends, family members, or other people who can give you continuing emotional support.

Know who and what you are fighting. Accurate information is important so victims can take effective action. Page 62, Useful Addresses and Internet Sites, provides information about hate groups and how to fight them.

Research your legal rights. More and more laws exist that severely punish perpetrators of hate. You may find it easier than you think to bring someone to court.

Remember that the hate crime is *not* your fault. You are not to blame.

Helping a Victim

A family member or friend may be a target of hate. You may know someone who is a victim of hate. You may have heard of someone in your community or in the news. Victims of hate often feel alone and open to attack. Other peoples' silence increases their sense of being alone. Your support means a great deal to them. Strong, quick support and small acts of kindness are valuable to victims.

For example, an African American family in an all-white neighborhood in Montgomery, Alabama, had received hate mail. A woman left them a rose and a note that said, "You are not alone."

In another example, a hate group was marching in Coeur d'Alene, Idaho. During the march, a group of neighbors invited several Hispanic and African American families to dinner. One host said it was just "a way of saying 'you are welcome.'"

Help victims decide to report the crime. If they are afraid of the legal system, offer to go with them to the police station or courthouse.

Points to Consider

Do you think fear is a good reason to avoid reporting a hate crime? Why or why not?

Do you agree that hate crimes are not simply mischief or careless fun? Why or why not?

Would you report a hate crime if you were a victim? Why or why not?

List some other ways you could provide strong, quick support to a victim of a hate crime.

Chapter Overview

Canada and the United States have made efforts to decrease hate crime.

Independent organizations are leaders in opposing hate.

Several successful lawsuits have been brought against hate groups for their members' criminal activities.

The Internet is being used to oppose hate groups' messages.

Counseling can help change people's attitude.

Chapter **6**

Government and Independent Efforts Against Hate

U.S. and Canadian Government Efforts

Lawmakers, government agencies, and public interest groups constantly seek better ways to identify hate crimes and their causes. They want to control conditions that appear to encourage or provoke hate crimes. The following are some of the efforts that governments have made.

"Laws against . . . hate propaganda are reasonable limits on freedom of expression because they prevent harm to individuals and groups."—From Section II of the Canadian Charter of Rights and Freedoms

In Canada

The following are some efforts the Canadian government has made to stop hate crimes.

Parliament has passed laws with stiff penalties for hate criminals.

The federal government works with other governments to prevent printed hate materials from passing among countries.

Canadian laws prohibit the promotion of hatred.

In the United States

Like Canada, the United States has made many efforts to oppose hate. Here are some of them.

The Juvenile Justice Office now keeps records on young hate criminals. It hopes to identify patterns in criminal behavior. Such knowledge may help prevent similar behavior in others.

School officials are trained to resolve conflict among members of different racial and ethnic groups.

The state of California has set up 10 regional networks to combat hate crimes. A social service agency is at the core of each network. Several committees report to the agency. The networks handle different areas, including community action, criminal justice, schools, the media, and young people.

The U.S. Congress has passed several laws to combat hate crimes. Some laws require each state to provide a plan for preventing young people from committing hate crimes.

To fight hate, it is helpful to know how many hate crimes are committed. For that reason, Congress has passed the Hate Crime Statistics Act. It requires the Attorney General's office to keep records of hate crime.

The FBI's Uniform Crime Report Division trains police nationwide in collecting hate crime data.

Other U.S. Efforts

The U.S. government has taken other steps to decrease hate. The Department of Education has given millions of dollars to community programs that help reduce tension among different groups. The Office of Juvenile Justice and Delinquency Prevention provides classes for young people in appreciating people's differences. The Justice Department's Office for Victims of Crime funds a special training program for law enforcement officers. It helps them learn to deal with hate crimes.

The U.S. Congress passed the Violence Against Women Act in 1994. The act funds improved law enforcement, shelters for battered women, and rape crisis centers. It includes clearer definitions of crimes against females. The act also allows victims of gender-based crimes to sue the perpetrators in federal court.

Presently, the U.S. Congress is considering a law to change federal hate crimes standards. Currently, a person may be arrested and tried for crimes based on race, religion, or national origin. The new law would allow the government to put criminals on trial for crimes based on sexual orientation, gender, or disability.

Encouraging New Numbers

According to the National Criminal Justice Association, 40 states have passed laws against hate-based violence and intimidation. The policies of 19 states call for the collection of data on hate crimes. Most of the remaining states have at least some form of laws against hate crime.

Independent Efforts

Along with governments, independent organizations are leading the fight against hate. For example, the Southern Poverty Law Center (SPLC) has brought several lawsuits against hate groups. The SPLC won multimillion-dollar judgments against the White Aryan Resistance and the Ku Klux Klan.

Several successful lawsuits have been brought against hate groups for setting fire to African American churches in the South. These court decisions are important because the organizations were held responsible for the crimes of their members. Such decisions may discourage hate groups from committing or promoting hate crimes.

The National Gay and Lesbian Task Force (NGLTF) has helped develop antiviolence materials for bisexual, gay, transsexual and lesbian groups. The NGLTF has tried to persuade lawmakers to include homosexual people among groups protected from hate crimes.

Several religious groups are working to promote racial and cultural tolerance. For instance, the Racial Reconciliation Initiative publishes materials to help Christians understand the differences among races. It identifies areas that might lead to conflict among members of different races. These areas include customs, language, and social structures.

The Anti-Defamation League (ADL) offers many programs to educate youth about hate crime. For instance, the ADL and other agencies developed the Youth Diversion Project in Massachusetts. In this program, young perpetrators can choose not to go to prison. Instead, they can attend alternative schools or take part in community service programs. This education is meant to draw these young people away from hate groups.

Computer software is available to block access to Internet sites that encourage violence toward specific groups.

The ADL also has created model laws to deal with hate crimes. This model calls for severe punishment if a crime is based on race, religion, gender, or sexual orientation. The ADL model also increases penalties for vandalism of houses of worship, cemeteries, schools, and community centers. At present, 40 U.S. states have laws patterned on the ADL model.

The ADL and a Boston TV station began the World of Difference campaign. It teaches students to face their own prejudice. At the same time, students learn to enjoy and celebrate people's differences. A World of Difference has become an international organization devoted to educating people in different settings.

Countering Hate on the Internet

Many efforts are being made to stop or oppose the presence of hate groups on the Internet. Because of First Amendment protection, U.S. hate groups can say anything they like. Rather than try to stop these groups, some organizations use the Internet to spread messages that oppose hate. Other organizations simply track hate groups and their Internet activities.

Two such groups are HateWatch and the National Association for the Advancement of Colored People (NAACP) Online. The NAACP was formed to ensure equality for all minority groups in the United States. These groups keep records and regularly report on hate groups' Internet sites. Such tracking can give authorities evidence in any future acts of crime that hate groups commit.

Governments are concerned about the spread of hate through the Internet. For instance, the Canadian government works with leaders of other countries to oppose the use of the Internet to spread hate.

Some groups have Internet programs to provide legal help for people who are victims of hate. For example, the Leadership Conference on Civil Rights gives free legal referrals over the Internet to victims of hate crime.

Counseling Hate Criminals

Counseling can help broaden the views of members of hate groups. After intensive counseling, members may be brought together with members of groups they have targeted. For instance, one program involved skinheads in Orange County, California. In addition to having three days of counseling, these people met with Holocaust survivors. Several skinheads changed their behavior as a result. The ADL has reported similar success with its counseling programs. People can learn and change. Some people's tendency to hate may disappear as their mind and outlook mature.

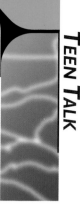
"When I went into counseling, I was ready to tell everybody all the good reasons I had to hate Jews. But then I got in the same room with some of them. I hadn't ever been with real Jews before. All of a sudden, I could see them not just as Jews, but as actual people."
—Martin, age 18

Points to Consider

Which do you think is more effective against hate crime—individuals or government programs? Why?

Do you think groups should be held responsible for crimes their members commit? Why or why not?

Do you think using the Internet to counter hate on the Internet is useful? Why or why not?

Chapter
Overview

Individuals can do much to curb hate.

People who oppose hate can work for positive change.

Educating children is the best way to stop hate.

Chapter **7**

Individual Efforts to Oppose Hate

Ray's mother has Swiss ancestors.
His father has a Scottish background.

RAY, AGE 16

Ray doesn't feel likely to be a target of hate. However, several of Ray's friends have been victims of hate crimes. He knows his friends have been targeted because of their African, Asian, Jewish, or Hispanic background. At times Ray feels guilty for being white. It's like some angry white people are giving the whole race a bad reputation.

Ray believes that the best thing he can do is to show that he doesn't hate anyone. He tries to understand his friends' customs and background better. He volunteers to teach kids of different cultures to read. He also helps to teach immigrants how to speak English.

Individuals Can Make a Difference

Besides reporting instances of hate, individuals can do other things to reduce it. You may think prejudice is so widespread that you can do nothing to limit it. That's not the case. Consider these important ways that you can lessen prejudice.

Find out how you are like rather than different from other people. Learn to value differences in race, religion, gender, or sexual orientation.

Get to know people who have different racial or ethnic backgrounds. Ignorance is a big part of hatred against others who are different. You can erase ignorance by learning about people as individuals, not as members of a group.

Spend time with people who have a different sexual orientation from yours. Get to know and appreciate them as individuals.

Think for yourself and form your own opinions rather than believe other people's hateful ideas.

Tell school authorities or police about hate group activities at school.

Let people know that you don't appreciate jokes based on race, gender, or sexual orientation.

Look into having your school's food service feature ethnic foods at mealtimes. This is another way to value differences.

Paint over racist graffiti.

Create a school flag or poster with symbols that celebrate diversity.

Film or write anti-hate commercials.

Interview teachers about their ethnic or racial background. Ask them about ways their background has influenced their experiences.

Ask the school or public library to set aside a diversity corner. It can feature books, magazines, and other publications from around the world.

Avoid lashing out at people who are different. You may temporarily feel better or stronger, but lashing out will not improve life for you or others.

Warn family and friends about hate propaganda on the Internet. Such misleading information can be damaging to many people. Some people may believe the propaganda.

Walk away from people who promote hate crimes.

Tell people who promote a racial stereotype that they are wrong.

"If you can teach a kid to realize what he's doing before it happens, you're going to save a lot of people."—Steve, age 15

You may have thought about getting together with friends to do a project that opposes hate. Here are five steps for group projects.

1. Decide on your project. List problems that you believe your group can change. Choose one problem. For example, is there racist graffiti that makes people feel afraid?

2. Make a step-by-step plan. Decide who will do what. Set deadlines for each step in your plan. Also plan for how to tell if your project is successful.

3. Get what you need. This includes getting materials and people to do the work. Don't forget transportation, meeting space, food, photocopies, money, publicity, and adult support. Start your project.

4. Check your progress. You want to see if what you are doing is working. Ask people what they think. For example, do they feel safer with neighborhood patrols that report graffiti? Count things. For example, if you intend to reduce graffiti, count how many walls had it before the project began. Compare that number to how many walls have it now.

5. Get the message out. Tell people what you're doing and ask them to help. When you're done, share your success in your school or local newspaper. Don't forget to celebrate.

Guiding Children

The best hope for fighting hate lies with educating children. They aren't born to hate others. They learn to hate. It is also true that children can learn not to hate. When enough children learn to accept the differences in people, then hate crimes will decrease.

You can strongly influence children's attitudes. Talk with them. Truthfully answer their questions. Here are suggestions to prevent prejudice in children. You may have additional ideas.

Stress the fact that prejudice and discrimination are unfair.

Tell children that some people are unfairly insulted and hated because of their skin color. National origin, religion, gender, or sexual orientation are other reasons people are hated.

Say that people sometimes can't get jobs, loans, or educational opportunities because of their background and beliefs. These factors sometimes keep people out of neighborhoods, social events, and clubs, too.

As children notice differences in others, discourage negative judgments about those people.

"Racism is a learned affliction and anything that is learned can be unlearned."—Jane Elliot

Discuss qualities that are important in friends. Let children know that appearances or differences are not important. Teach them that it's what's inside that counts.

Make each child feel unique and special. Children who feel good about themselves are less likely to put others down.

Help children become sensitive to other people's feelings. Children who have this kind of sensitivity will more likely accept other people and their differences.

Setting a Good Example

Don't stop there. You may have heard the saying "Actions speak louder than words." This means that children will learn as much from what you do as what you say. Be a good role model. It's up to everyone to stop hate. You can take the first step.

Carmetta believes that she has always been the oddball. Her

CARMETTA, AGE 16

friends seem to have rules for what to do and who to do it with. However, Carmetta thinks for herself. People may criticize her, but she knows that she can do as she likes with her life.

Carmetta has refused to stick with people just like her. She has been friends with all kinds of different people. She has white, Hispanic, and Asian friends. She has friends from many religious backgrounds. Carmetta thinks it's great that North America has people from so many backgrounds. She believes that plain old ignorance causes fear or dislike of people who are different. The more people know about each other, the less they will hate.

Points to Consider

Do you think individuals can fight hate? Explain.

How could you overcome your own negative feelings about people of a certain group?

If someone you knew were a victim of a hate crime, what could you say to him or her? Explain.

Do you think children learn as much from your behavior as from your words? Why or why not?

Glossary

anti-Semitism (an-tee-SEM-uh-tizm)—hatred of Jewish people

bisexual (bye-SEK-shoo-wuhl)—relating to the sexual attraction of a person to both males and females

discrimination (diss-krim-uh-NAY-shuhn)—unfair treatment of people based on prejudice against them

gay (GAY)—homosexual; usually refers to males who have homosexual attractions.

genocide (JEN-uh-side)—the planned murder of an entire racial, political, or cultural group

hate speech (HATE SPEECH)—spoken or printed insults aimed at a particular group

homosexual (hoh-moh-SEK-shoo-wuhl)—relating to the desire for, attraction to, and/or sexual involvement with a person of the same gender

intimidate (in-TIM-uh-dayt)—to frighten or bully someone

lesbian (LEZ-bee-uhn)—homosexual; usually refers to females who have homosexual attractions.

perpetrator (PUR-puh-tray-tur)—someone who commits a crime

persecute (PUR-suh-kyoot)—to continually attack and mistreat

prejudice (PREJ-uh-diss)—an unfair opinion or prejudgment about a person or group

propaganda (prop-uh-GAN-duh)—sometimes misleading information; propaganda is meant to influence people or damage enemies.

sexual orientation (SEK-shoo-wuhl or-ee-uhn-TAY-shuhn)—sexual attractions, behavior, or desire for other people based on their gender

stereotype (STER-ee-oh-tipe)—an overly simple idea or opinion of a person, group, or thing

transsexual (tran-SEK-shoo-wuhl)—relating to a male who feels like a female, or a female who feels like a male

For More Information

D'Angelo, Laura. *Hate Crimes.* Philadelphia: Chelsea House, 1998.

Gedatus, Gus. *Gangs and Violence.* Mankato, MN: Capstone, 2000.

Gedatus, Gus. *Violence in Public Places.* Mankato, MN: Capstone, 2000.

Osborn, Kevin. *Bias Incidents.* New York: Rosen, 1997.

Winters, Paul. *Hate Crimes.* San Diego: Greenhaven, 1996.

Useful Addresses and Internet Sites

Anti-Defamation League (ADL)
823 United Nations Plaza
New York, NY 10017
www.adl.org

Gay and Lesbian Alliance Against Defamation
www.glaad.org
1-800-GAY-MEDIA (1-800-429-6334)
Information about treatment of gay and lesbian people in U.S. society

Horizons Anti-Violence Project
961 West Montana
Chicago, IL 60614

Parents, Families, and Friends of Lesbians and Gays (PFLAG)
1101 14th Street, Northwest
Suite 1030
Washington, DC 20005
www.pflag.org

Southern Poverty Law Center
400 Washington Avenue
Montgomery, AL 36104
www.splcenter.org

BlackFamilies.com
http://blackfamilies.com/living/family_relation ships/hate_crimes.html
Information on avoiding and fighting hate groups

Matthew's Place
www.matthewsplace.com
Updates and background on the murder trial of Russell Henderson and Aaron McKinney; other resources for gay and lesbian people

National Multicultural Institute
www.nmci.org
Links to multicultural Internet sites

United States Department of Justice—Justice for Kids
www.usdoj.gov/kidspage/getinvolved
Ideas to get involved in crime prevention of all kinds

WePrevent.Org
www.weprevent.org
Ideas to help prevent violence

YWCA
http://38.202.2.16/html/B4b5a1a.asp
Ideas about how to fight hate against females and other minority groups

Index

Index continued